TOUCHING
THE SUPERNATURAL WORLD
Angels, Miracles, & Demons

RELIGION & MODERN CULTURE
Title List

TOUCHING
THE SUPERNATURAL WORLD
Angels, Miracles, & Demons

by Kenneth McIntosh, M.Div.,
and Marsha McIntosh

Mason Crest Publishers
Philadelphia

Mason Crest Publishers Inc.
370 Reed Road
Broomall, Pennsylvania 19008
(866) MCP-BOOK (toll free)

First printing
1 2 3 4 5 6 7 8 9 10

Library of Congress Cataloging-in-Publication Data

McIntosh, Kenneth, 1959–
  Touching the supernatural world : angels, miracles, and demons / by Kenneth McIntosh and Marsha McIntosh.
     p. cm. — (Religion and modern culture)
  Includes index.
  ISBN 1-59084-981-7   ISBN 1-59084-970-1 (series)
  1. Supernatural. I. McIntosh, Marsha. II. Title. III. Series.
  BL100.M29 2006
  202'.1—dc22

                    2005007632

Produced by Harding House Publishing Service, Inc.
www.hardinghousepages.com
Interior design by Dianne Hodack.
Cover design by MK Bassett-Harvey.
Printed in India.

CONTENTS

INTRODUCTION

by Dr. Marcus J. Borg

You are about to begin an important and exciting experience: the study of modern religion. Knowing about religion—and religions—is vital for understanding our neighbors, whether they live down the street or across the globe.

Despite the modern trend toward religious doubt, most of the world's population continues to be religious. Of the approximately six billion people alive today, around two billion are Christians, one billion are Muslims, 800 million are Hindus, and 400 million are Buddhists. Smaller numbers are Sikhs, Shinto, Confucian, Taoist, Jewish, and indigenous religions.

Religion plays an especially important role in North America. The United States is the most religious country in the Western world: about 80 percent of Americans say that religion is "important" or "very important" to them. Around 95 percent say they believe in God. These figures are very different in Europe, where the percentages are much smaller. Canada is "in between": the figures are lower than for the United States, but significantly higher than in Europe. In Canada, 68 percent of citizens say religion is of "high importance," and 81 percent believe in God or a higher being.

The United States is largely Christian. Around 80 percent describe themselves as Christian. In Canada, professing Christians are 77 percent of the population. But religious diversity is growing. According to Harvard scholar Diana Eck's recent book *A New Religious America*, the United States has recently become the most religiously diverse country in the world. Canada is also a country of great religious variety.

Fifty years ago, religious diversity in the United States meant Protestants, Catholics, and Jews, but since the 1960s, immigration from Asia, the Middle East, and Africa has dramatically increased the number of people practicing other religions. There are now about six million Muslims, four million Buddhists, and a million Hindus in the United States. To compare these figures to two historically important Protestant denominations in the United States, about 3.5 million are Presbyterians and 2.5 million are Episcopalians. There are more Buddhists in the United States than either of these denominations, and as many Muslims as the two denominations combined. This means that knowing about other religions is not just knowing about people in other parts of the world—but about knowing people in our schools, workplaces, and neighborhoods.

Moreover, religious diversity does not simply exist between religions. It is found within Christianity itself:

• There are many different forms of Christian worship. They range from Quaker silence to contemporary worship with rock music to traditional liturgical worship among Catholics and Episcopalians to Pentecostal enthusiasm and speaking in tongues.

- Christians are divided about the importance of an afterlife. For some, the next life—a paradise beyond death—is their primary motive for being Christian. For other Christians, the afterlife does not matter nearly as much. Instead, a relationship with God that transforms our lives this side of death is the primary motive.
- Christians are divided about the Bible. Some are biblical literalists who believe that the Bible is to be interpreted literally and factually as the inerrant revelation of God, true in every respect and true for all time. Other Christians understand the Bible more symbolically as the witness of two ancient communities—biblical Israel and early Christianity—to their life with God.

Christians are also divided about the role of religion in public life. Some understand "separation of church and state" to mean "separation of religion and politics." Other Christians seek to bring Christian values into public life. Some (commonly called "the Christian Right") are concerned with public policy issues such as abortion, prayer in schools, marriage as only heterosexual, and pornography. Still other Christians name the central public policy issues as American imperialism, war, economic injustice, racism, health care, and so forth. For the first group, values are primarily concerned with individual behavior. For the second group, values are also concerned with group behavior and social systems. The study of religion in North America involves not only becoming aware of other religions but also becoming aware of differences within Christianity itself. Such study can help us to understand people with different convictions and practices.

And there is one more reason why such study is important and exciting: religions deal with the largest questions of life. These questions are intellectual, moral, and personal. Most centrally, they are:

- What is real? The religions of the world agree that "the real" is more than the space-time world of matter and energy.
- How then shall we live?
- How can we be "in touch" with "the real"? How can we connect with it and become more deeply centered in it?

This series will put you in touch with other ways of seeing reality and how to live.

AUTHORS' NOTE

The "modern-day" accounts in this book come from a variety of sources. Many came from books and magazines, some came from people we know, and a very few come from the authors' experiences. We have no way to verify each account. Even if we spoke with the people claiming these experiences, we still cannot know if they are telling the truth. Furthermore, supernatural events are a matter of personal interpretation. The best we can guarantee is that the stories are "true" according to their sources. Modern America is a spiritual hodgepodge, so we have attempted to present the experiences of a wide variety of people in today's culture.

This book concerns the supernatural. Supernatural events, by their definition, defy scientific proof. Do we, the authors, believe the stories in this book? Some we believe; we feel more skeptical about others. Sometimes, we do not know what to think. Like you, we make our choices based on our own worldview.

Chapter 1

SUPERNATURAL EXPERIENCES

RELIGION & MODERN CULTURE

Joe has been struggling lately. He has been agitated, irrationally angry with people. At this point, many people would visit a psychiatrist. Joe does something quite different: he attends a Bible study group associated with Victory Community Church, where Sam, the Bible study leader, gives Joe some unexpected advice.

"It sounds like demonic oppression."

"What do you mean?" Joe asks. "You mean like I'm possessed or something?"

"Not possessed," Sam answers. "But spiritual forces do influence the way we live. The book of First Peter says, 'Your enemy the devil prowls around like a lion.' Now, we don't want to be paranoid—but spiritual teachers have known for centuries that evil powers do influence our lives. I think you should call Pastor Steve and see if he thinks *deliverance* ministry would help you."

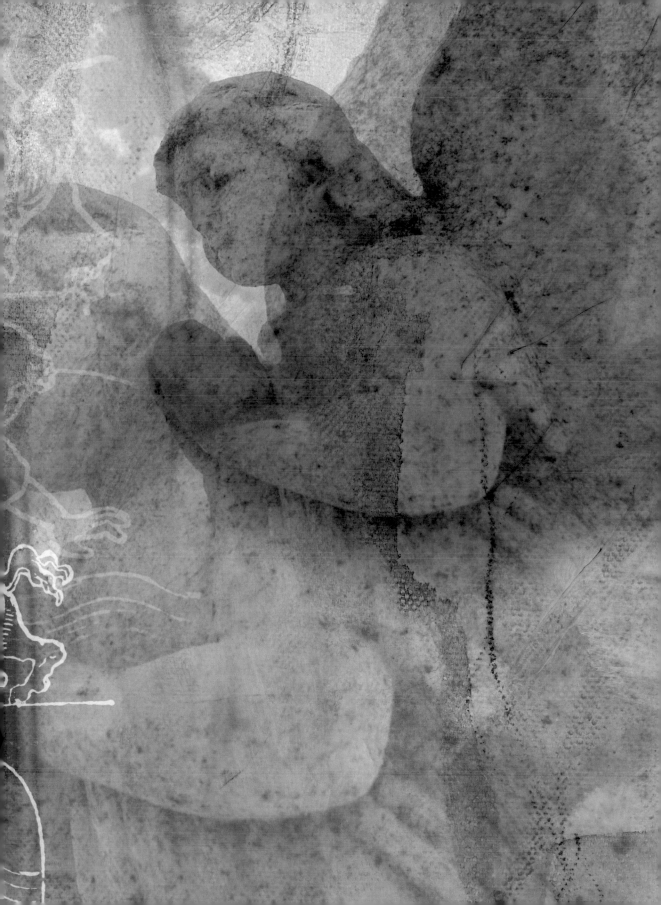

When Joe calls the pastor, Pastor Steve says, "I'd like to try and help you. Can you meet with me and another pastor Saturday morning?" Joe agrees.

Saturday morning, Joe meets at Pastor Steve's office. Pastor Tim, an assistant minister, is there also. Pastor Steve explains the procedure. "Joe, I don't want you to think anyone is accusing you of being evil or especially sinful. The fact is, the devil is constantly seeking to corrupt and destroy believers' lives. Maybe that's what you're experiencing. We're going to talk and pray with you. If a spirit manifests—if it begins to communicate with us directly—we'll take charge. Now, let's begin by all agreeing in prayer that Jesus Christ is Lord of our lives."

They bow their heads and pray. Then the pastors take turns praying for God to free Joe from spiritual forces that are oppressing him. In the middle of their prayers, Joe starts laughing—but the voice does not sound like Joe. It is sarcastic and full of hate.

"You idiots! You fools! You can't tell us what to do. We've been with Joe for a long time now. He's ours."

Pastor Steve assumes a stern tone. "Spirits, we command you by the shed blood of Jesus Christ to leave this man at once!"

The voice shouts back, cursing the pastors. The two ministers continue to speak forcefully. "Spirits of *condemnation* and spirits of profanity, we command you in Jesus's name to leave this man *now!*"

Joe becomes silent, and slumps quietly into his seat. He stares at the two pastors with a confused, frightened expression. Steve and Tim glance at one another.

"Joe, do you remember what just happened?" Pastor Steve asks gently.

Joe shakes his head. "It's like I lost time or something . . . everything seems foggy."

Pastor Steve nods. "It's as we suspected—you've been oppressed by evil spirits. We commanded them to leave, and they're gone now. We need to talk about some principles of spiritual warfare, so evil forces won't be able to gain this kind of influence over your life in the future."

GLOSSARY

astrology: The practice of predicting the future by looking at the stars.

charismatic: A branch of Christianity that emphasizes supernatural events in the modern day.

condemnation: Casting guilt upon someone.

deliverance: A term used by evangelicals to refer to the removal of demonic influences from a person's life.

dualistic worldview: Belief in two worlds, the visible and the invisible.

enchanted worldview: Belief that all natural objects and creatures have a spiritual nature.

evangelical: A branch of Christianity that holds a high view of the Bible's authority and the necessity of a personal relationship with Jesus Christ.

exorcisms: Rituals of special prayers used to rid someone of demonic influence.

integrated worldviews: A combination of differing beliefs put together to form a new worldview; also called postmodern worldview.

materialistic worldview: The belief that only material things are real; also called scientific worldview.

mystical: Having a spiritual meaning that is neither apparent to the senses nor obvious to the intelligence.

New Agers: People who believe in a cultural movement that emphasizes spiritual consciousness and often involves belief in reincarnation, astrology, and the practice of meditation.

pantheism: The belief that God is in all natural things.

postmodern: A movement developed in response to the modern movement; it often includes a return to classical elements.

RELIGION & MODERN CULTURE

"There are more things in heaven and earth,
Horatio, than are dreamt of in your philosophy."
—*from* Hamlet, *by William Shakespeare*

Joe gulps, and nods. He is absolutely convinced that he has experienced a supernatural problem.

SUPERNATURAL BELIEFS IN NORTH AMERICA TODAY

Some people would think the scene above sounds like fantasy. The names and specifics have been changed to maintain confidentiality, but the general description is an authentic depiction of things that happen in some religious circles. Deliverance sessions of this sort occur in certain *evangelical* and *charismatic* churches. Roman Catholic churches engage less often in deliverance ministry, and use somewhat different techniques—but they also have practiced *exorcisms* for centuries. If you were to tape a deliverance session, you would see that persons allegedly under demonic influence sometimes do speak in altered voices, and on occasion, they will act in ways very different from their normal personalities.

You might have different ideas of what is happening depending on your background. If you think only in terms of a scientific worldview, you might suggest that Joe has multiple personality disorder, which is a psychological problem. If you are very skeptical, you would probably say Joe is playing a game and making it all up. If you believe in the supernatural, you might say an evil spirit has oppressed Joe. Alternatively, you might think a combination of supernatural and psychological factors are at work here; perhaps some kind of destructive spiritual energy has influenced Joe's thinking.

In the modern scientific world, you might think that very few people would believe in demonic possession and miraculous deliverances. The fact is, however, millions of Americans believe in angels, miracles, and demons. They believe the supernatural world is real. In twenty-first-century America, it is more "normal" to believe in the supernatural than not.

One out of every five U.S. residents believes he or she has seen an angel or knows someone who has, according to a survey of 1,127 adult residents of the United States conducted by Scripps Howard News Service and Ohio University. Seventy-seven percent of adults in the poll answered yes to the question: "Do you believe angels, that is, some kind of heavenly beings who visit Earth, in fact exist?" Another 73 percent believe angels still "come into the world even in these modern days."

Furthermore, the great majority of U.S. citizens believe in miracles. The May 1, 2000, issue of *Newsweek* featured an article on miracle claims ("What Miracles Mean" by Kenneth L. Woodward) that incorporated data from a *Newsweek* poll conducted by Princeton Survey Research Associates. The poll showed that:

- 84 percent of Americans said that God performs miracles.
- 79 percent accept the accounts of miracles in the Bible as accurate.
- 72 percent said that "People who face death in accidents or natural disasters can be saved by a miracle."
- Two-thirds of Americans say that they have prayed for a miracle.

Furthermore, a majority of Americans believes in evil spiritual beings. In 2001, both Gallup and Harris polls revealed that 68 percent of American adults believe in the devil. That is the largest percentage of belief in spiritual evil since 1950. An earlier survey showed that people who believe in Satan divide fifty-fifty on the nature of the devil. Half be-

CANADIAN BELIEFS

In general, Canadians appear to be less religious than U.S. citizens. Only half as many Canadians go to church weekly as do residents of the United States. At the same time, belief in supernatural or unexplained phenomena is significant in Canada. Forty-five percent of Canadians pray daily. Forty-three percent believe in out-of-body experiences. Thirty-seven percent believe in ghosts. When asked the reason for their belief in the supernatural or paranormal, almost one in four said their reason was "personal experience."

lieve the devil is a personal being, and half believe the devil is "an impersonal force." Yet a majority of Americans agrees that he (or it) influences the world negatively.

All different kinds of Americans believe in the supernatural. Male and female, young and old, African American, Caucasian, Asian, Latino, and American Indian—in every racial and cultural group you will find believers in supernatural reality. Belief in supernatural experiences is not limited to any single religion. Muslims, Buddhists, Jews, *New Agers*, and Christians all report supernatural experiences.

"To see a World in a Grain of Sand
And a Heaven in a Wild Flower,
Hold Infinity in the palm of your hand
And Eternity in an hour."
—*William Blake*

WORLDVIEWS DETERMINE HOW WE INTERPRET WHAT WE EXPERIENCE

When looking at the San Francisco Peaks, people see different things even though they are viewing the same object. The Peaks rise 12,500 feet (3,810 meters) into the sky over Flagstaff, Arizona. Clouds often hover on the top of the mountain. This happens even on days when the rest of the sky is completely clear. Sometimes, rainbows will reach across the sky, seeming to end right at the tip of the mountain.

A family of Native American heritage lives close to the mountain. They see the mountain through traditional eyes. They believe powerful spiritual forces inhabit the place. Looking at the mountain, this family sees the image of a Kokopeli (a spirit being, who plays a flute) in the formations of rock and snow. They look at the mountain from an ***enchanted worldview***.

Another local resident is highly educated in the natural sciences. He can explain how millions of years ago molten materials from the earth's core pushed up through the crust, forming the volcanic mountain. He explains that the mountains have an unusual, self-contained water cycle. This causes the cloud cover and rainbows. He looks at the mountain mostly from a ***materialistic worldview***.

Every person has a worldview—a collection of beliefs about life and the universe. How an individual interprets life will depend on her worldview. One person might say he saw an angel—while another might explain it as a hallucination, or as someone pulling a trick.

Many different influences form a person's worldview. An individual's culture and family have great influence on what he believes. Do they come from a religious background? Do they believe in the supernatural? Movies and television will also influence a person's worldview. Does he watch *Joan of Arcadia* or *It's a Miracle*? How about the Discovery Channel or the *X-Files*? Each of these programs communicates a different worldview.

Experiences also influence worldview. For example, a woman whose father left her family when she was very young believes God is distant and uncaring. Another person believes she saw a ghost when she was a little girl. The experience was very vivid and made her open to all sorts of supernatural beliefs. Each person forms his or her own unique worldview based on background and experiences.

FOUR WORLDVIEWS

Worldview is one of those topics where there seem to be three opinions every time you get two experts together. Definitions vary. So do the categories. Many experts, however, agree that four worldviews are the most common.

A WORLD OF ENCHANTMENT

The enchanted worldview is common among tribal societies that live close to nature. It is closely associated with **pantheism**—the belief that God or gods are in all things. In this view, *every thing in nature is a spiritual being*. A mountain, a stream, a deer, and a dog—each is a spirit being.

Groups of New Age believers travel to Cathedral Rock in Sedona, Arizona. They build shrines out of stones, and then stand with their arms outstretched so they can feel the energy formed by supernatural vortexes. They are displaying belief in an enchanted world.

THE TRUTH IS OUT THERE

One of the most popular television series of the 1990s was the *X-Files*. Each week, the *X-Files'* characters explored supernatural mysteries. Fox Mulder was open to everything. The sign on his office wall said, "I want to believe." A UFO abducted his sister, and he spent his life trying to discover the truth behind paranormal, supernatural, and extraterrestrial events. His partner, Dana Sculley, on the other hand, was a trained scientist. She assumed logical, common-sense explanations for strange events. Mulder and Sculley constantly disagreed about what they saw and experienced. This delighted audiences, who recognized in Mulder and Sculley their own struggles between skepticism and belief. At the end of the final episode, Sculley said she had found the greatest force in the universe—and the camera zoomed in to show her clutching a cross. It was an affirmation that many Americans, whether they are skeptical or accepting of supernatural experiences, still find solace in religious faith.

A dualistic worldview divides reality into two parts: the natural and the supernatural worlds.

Other people consult their horoscope every day. *Astrology* assumes that the stars have spiritual power to influence mortal lives. This is another example of an enchanted worldview.

TWO WORLDS

The *dualistic worldview* dominated the Western world for more than a thousand years. "Dual" means "two." *A dualistic worldview divides reality into two parts: the natural and the supernatural worlds.* The natural world is visible and tangible (we can physically touch it). It includes the earth, animals, and natural substances. The supernatural world is invisible and people can only experience it by religious or *mystical* experience. This supernatural world includes God, heaven, the devil, angels, and demons. This perspective is rooted in Greek philosophy, Judaism, Christianity, and Islam. Many people who follow these faiths, however, also hold other worldviews as well.

According to a dualistic worldview, the visible and invisible worlds may be very close to one another, but they rarely touch. They are set up like a one-way mirror. Beings that live in the supernatural world (God, angels, and demons) are able to view beings in the natural world. Humans, however, are only rarely able to see into the supernatural realm. This occurs occasionally in the form of visions—for example, an appearance of the Virgin Mary. The natural world only glimpses the supernatural world when supernatural beings decide to allow it. If a person prays to God or asks favors from a saint, she may be showing belief in a dualistic worldview. She does not see the one to whom she speaks, but she believes the saint or God hears her in the invisible realm.

A SCIENTIFIC WORLD

The materialistic worldview was strongest during the twentieth century, especially in Europe and communist states. This view reduces reality to the natural world. The materialistic worldview is closely associated with science. Scientists draw conclusions only after they have weighed, measured, and reproduced things, so science cannot document spiritual matters. Of course, some scientists hold spiritual beliefs. They combine a materialistic worldview with other worldviews.

A COMBINATION OF WORLDS

Finally, some people hold **integrated worldviews**. These perspectives are most common today. An integrated worldview combines one or more of the views above. Writers sometimes call this a **postmodern** worldview. The "modern" view was common during the twentieth century and was exclusively materialistic. The twenty-first century is "post" (after) the modern era, and it includes a variety of views. For example, an individual may believe the scientific view of human evolution yet also believe God controlled the evolutionary process. A 1991 Gallup poll found that 40 percent of Americans believe that God created human life and used the process of evolution to do so. That belief integrates (combines) both materialistic and dualistic worldviews.

A UCLA professor claimed no religious belief—and yet he believed he had experienced a miracle. When an auto accident threw him from his car, he lay in the middle of the road with serious injuries. He heard a voice, very clear, saying to him, "Move off the road—you must move off the road or you'll be killed." He looked around, but no one was there. He was all alone on the road. Yet he heard the voice very clearly. He mustered his strength and pulled his damaged body to the roadside. Moments later, a vehicle sped past him. According to this professor, if he had not heeded the voice from an invisible being, he would be dead.

25

FORMING A WORLDVIEW: FROM ATHEIST TO BORN-AGAIN

Highly educated, scientific parents raised a son in California. They reared him to believe their materialistic worldview. By the time he reached college, he was an atheist—a person who did not believe in God.

At college, he began doing drugs. On an acid trip, he had a shocking experience. He says, "I saw the devil." This was different from any other trip he ever had. He saw this thing clearly, as if he was fully alert and he could touch it. He beheld a creature that was utterly evil, utterly hateful, and horrifically frightening. When he came out of the trip, his first words were, "Man, there is a devil. He is real, and I saw him. I just pray there's a God too, or I'm a goner."

For the first time in his life, he began looking at religion. Today, he is a "born-again" Christian. His worldview changed because of a single powerful experience.

The majority of people who claim supernatural experiences see things that fit their own worldview.

The professor did not know how to explain the event. He was not religious, but he was convinced something supernatural spared his life.

As we said earlier, a person's experiences form her worldview—but at the same time, *a person's worldview influences what she experiences*. For example, the Virgin Mary seems to appear exclusively to Catholics. Very few Protestant Christians, Hindus, or Muslims have experienced a visitation from the Virgin Mary. Likewise, born-again Christians are unlikely to experience visionary messages from the Hindu deity Lord Krishna. But Krishna does appear to Hindus. There are exceptions to this rule, such as skeptics like the UCLA professor who admit to apparently supernatural experiences. Nonetheless, the majority of people who claim supernatural experiences see things that fit their own worldview.

In a January 2004 poll, 91 percent of Americans said they believe in some form of supernatural reality. Even as technology increases and our world becomes more sophisticated, more and more Americans incorporate the unseen world into their worldview.

Chapter 2

ANGELS
IN SACRED SCRIPTURES

Hagar was desperate. Her master had sent her into the desert with her young son. Where would they go? The sun was so hot. How would they survive with only a single canteen of water and a little bread?

The trouble had started a while back. Hagar's mistress, Sarah, had been trying for years to have a child. If there was no child, who would carry on the family line? Finally, her mistress came up with a plan. She insisted her husband have a baby with Hagar, the household servant. This was a step up for a maid. She was no longer just a servant girl but part of the family.

The angels . . . regard our safety, undertake our defense, direct our ways, and exercise a constant solicitude that no evil befalls us.

—*John Calvin*

Looking back, she wished she had hid her delight a little more when she had gotten pregnant. Maybe she had flaunted it a little too much to her mistress. Later when a miracle happened and the elderly mistress also had a son, Sarah did not like having the maid and her child around.

Now what were they to do? Their food and water were all gone. They were in the middle of nowhere.

The mother put her son under a bush and sat a distance away. She could do nothing but cry.

Suddenly she heard the voice of an angel. He said God had heard her son crying out for help. The angel instructed her to lift up the boy and hold him fast with her hand. God would make a great nation from him—the Arab nation. God opened her eyes and she saw a well close by to satisfy their thirst.

This story comes from the Jewish Torah and the Christian Bible. It tells about Hagar, her son Ishmael, and her master and mistress—Abraham and Sarah—and an angel! It is one of many accounts of angelic beings bringing messages of hope and help to human beings.

Arabs today regard Hagar's child by Abraham, Ishmael, as their ancestor. Jews regard Abraham's other child, Isaac, as their ancestor. God promised Abraham his children would inherit the Promised Land. To this day, Jewish Israelis and Arab Palestinians—each claiming descent from Abraham—fight over the land promised to his children. At the same time, many organizations urge Arabs and Jews to unite in recognition of their common ancestor. Abraham may be one key to peace in the Middle East. If that happened, many would regard the resulting peace as truly the work of angels.

GLOSSARY

cherubim: The plural word for "cherub." Although more modern mythology pictures a cherub as a fat little boy with wings, in biblical terminology, a cherub was something quite different. The cherubim were amazing creatures with four wings and four faces (human, lion, bull, and eagle).

dharma: In Buddhism, the truth about how things are and will always be.

djinns: In Islamic mythology, spirits that assume human and animal forms and make mischievous use of their supernatural powers.

shaitans: In Islamic belief, devils.

ANCIENT BELIEFS ABOUT ANGELS

Since the beginning of recorded history, traces of angelic beings appear in art, pictographs, and writings. Did the earliest humans experience angels? Were there Neanderthal angels?

Our earliest recordings of angels come from the Sumerian culture. Around 3000 BCE, the Sumerians lived in the region of present-day Iraq. They believed in "messengers" who went between humans and gods delivering messages. Archaeologists have found a stone picture called a stele in an excavation site; the picture shows a winged being descending

DATING SYSTEMS & THEIR MEANING

You might be accustomed to seeing dates expressed with the abbreviations BC or AD, as in the year 1000 BC or the year AD 1900. For centuries, this dating system has been the most common in the Western world. However, since BC and AD are based on Christianity (BC stands for Before Christ and AD stands for *anno Domini*, Latin for "in the year of our Lord"), many people now prefer to use abbreviations that people from all religions can be comfortable using. The abbreviations BCE (meaning Before Common Era) and CE (meaning Common Era) mark time in the same way (for example, 1000 BC is the same year as 1000 BCE, and AD 1900 is the same year as 1900 CE), but BCE and CE do not have the same religious overtones as BC and AD.

from one of seven heavens. The creature is pouring the water of life into the cup of the king. Some scholars believe this to be the earliest known likeness of an angel.

"The angel of the Lord encampeth around about them that fear him, delivereth them."

—*Psalm 34:7*

ANGELS IN BUDDHISM

Buddhists speak of *devas*, or celestial beings. Some schools of Buddhism also refer to *dharmapalas*, or **dharma** protectors. These are similar to angels in Western thought. Devas are spiritual beings described as bodies of light or energy. However, they are often portrayed in physical forms. According to the Web site Belief Net, "Devas normally do not interfere in human affairs, but as Buddhist teacher Lama Surya Das notes, they have been known to rejoice, applaud, and rain down flowers for good deeds performed in the world."

ANGELS IN THE HEBREW SCRIPTURES

Our English word "angel" comes from the Greek word *ággelos*, which means "messenger." The Hebrew word that most closely resembles the word angel is *mal'ach*, which also means "messenger."

Both Jews and Christians regard the books of the Hebrew Bible as sacred truth. In Hebrew, these scriptures are called Tanakh. Christians most often refer to these same scriptures as the Old Testament. The stories of the Hebrew Bible, so important to both religions, often describe God's actions in human history taking place through angels.

Jews call the first five books of the Hebrew Bible, said to be written by Moses, the Torah. The presence of angels in the Torah begins in the book of Genesis with Adam and Eve, the first humans. God placed them

"He will give his angels charge of you, to guard you in all your ways."

—*Psalm 90:11*

in paradise and told them they could eat from every tree and plant—except for one: they had to avoid the "tree of good and evil." In the ancient story, a serpent persuaded them, and they ate of the forbidden fruit. God saw that they had changed—they had become dangerous to the world and to each other. God put them out of the Garden of Eden and placed **cherubim**, a type of angel, to guard the gates of Eden. These angels served as heavenly bouncers.

The Hebrew scriptures tell how angels appeared many times to Abraham and his family. Three angels came to Abraham by the oaks of Mamre, in the Promised Land. These apparently ordinary men let Abraham wash their feet, and they ate food. One of the three angels was Yahweh—or God himself. He told Abraham that his elderly wife Sarah would have a son, and Abraham's descendants would be a great nation. Sarah laughed in scorn when she heard that she would have a child in her old age. Yet Sarah did have a son, and they named him Isaac, which means laughter.

One of these angels then told Abraham that God would destroy the twin cities of Sodom and Gomorrah for their pervasive wickedness. The book of Ezekiel explains that the citizens of Sodom "did not care for the poor and the needy, they were overfed and unconcerned." Abraham had a nephew, Lot, in that city, and Abraham was concerned for Lot's safety. Therefore, Abraham bargained with the angel to save the cities of Sodom and Gomorrah. He was unsuccessful, but two angels came to the city and literally pulled Lot and his family out of harm's way before the destruction began.

One of the most dramatic stories from the book of Genesis is when God told Abraham to sacrifice his son. Other ancient cultures practiced

GUARDIAN ANGELS

A bumper sticker reads, "Don't drive faster than your guardian angel can fly." Many North Americans believe they have guardian angels. Where does the notion of guardian angels come from? In the Christian Bible, it is found in Matthew 18:10: "Take care that you do not despise one of these little ones [children]; for, I tell you, in heaven their angels continually see the face of my Father in heaven." Another "guardian angel" verse in the New Testament is Hebrews 1:14: "Are they not all ministering spirits sent forth to minister for those who will inherit salvation?" The verse in Matthew only says that children each have an angel—it does not mention whether adults also have them. The verse in Hebrews does not specify that each person has an angel. However, some interpreters put the two passages together, forming the concept that each human has his or her own guardian angel.

child sacrifice, but not the Hebrews. According to the story, God told Abraham to take Isaac to an altar, cut his throat, and offer him to God. Abraham decided to obey God, even though his son was his most precious possession. He took Isaac, along with firewood and a knife, to a secluded place. Abraham built an altar, bound his son, and put him on it.

"It is not because angels are holier than men or devils that makes them angels, but because they do not expect holiness from one another, but from God alone."

—*William Blake*

He was ready to kill Isaac when the voice of an angel commanded him to stop—just in time. God was testing Abraham and was pleased with the old man's obedience.

Moses is a central figure in the Torah. He is the one who led God's chosen people out from the oppressive rule of the Egyptians, and he delivered the Ten Commandments. God spoke to Moses through a burning bush and told him to lead his people out of Egypt. The Torah says, "the angel of the Lord appeared to him in a flame of fire out of the midst of the bush."

ANGELS IN CHRISTIAN SCRIPTURES

In the Christian Gospels, Jesus experienced the presence of angels at crucial times in his life. When the time came for Jesus to enter the world, the angel Gabriel appeared to Mary of Nazareth and told her she was going to be pregnant with God's son. This caused problems for Mary's fiancé, Joseph. According to the Gospels of Matthew and Luke, Mary had not had sex with Joseph—or anyone else. Of course, that was difficult for Joseph to believe. People back then knew the facts of life as well as we do. But Matthew's Gospel says an angel then appeared to Joseph and explained how his bride-to-be was miraculously pregnant.

In a well-known passage, the Gospel of Luke says that angels announced the birth of Jesus to shepherds, saying, "Behold, I bring you

NATIVE AMERICAN ANGELS?

The connection between feathered wings and God's messengers may be cross-cultural. For instance, anthropologists surmise that Native American images of hawks and eagles, images that span many centuries, may symbolize beings that American Indians believed acted as spiritual messengers, intermediaries between the spirit world and human beings. Modern Native Americans often believe that spirit messengers appear in dreams and visions, helping people move correctly along their life path. Birds of prey are often seen as visual symbols of these sacred messengers, and feathers are worn or carried by Native Americans to connect them with spirit powers.

good tidings of great joy . . . unto you a Savior is born, Christ the Lord." Contrary to some well-known Christmas carols, the New Testament does not say the angels sang—they just announced. Some Bible scholars say that the angels' words have more meaning than most churchgoers realize. The titles they give Jesus are similar to the way that Roman citizens described their Caesar at that time. The Romans regarded their emperor as divine. The angels have a political message—it is Jesus, not Caesar, whom people should worship and obey.

Angels are present at Jesus's birth and at his rising from death. According to the Christian Gospels, the morning of the third day after

Jesus's death, some of his female followers went to his gravesite. They found an empty tomb and an angel. The angel shone like lightning with robes white as snow. He spoke to the women, telling them that Jesus had risen from the grave.

ANGELS IN ISLAM

Islam also calls angels messengers—*Malaika* in Arabic. They guard over humans and write down what they do. Islamic angels are not feminine or masculine. They guard the gates of heaven so that demons, *djinns*, and *shaitans* cannot "listen."

Mika'il (Michael) has wings of green topaz and yellow hair from head to toe. Each of his hairs has a million faces; in each face are a million eyes. Each eye sheds seventy thousand tears. His tears become the Kerubim (similar to the Hebrew word for cherubim), and they lean down over the trees, the fruit, the rain, and the flowers. In Mika'il's mouth are a million tongues, and each speaks a million languages. Can you imagine the sound this would make?

Djubril (Gabriel) is the angel who appeared to the Prophet Mohammed and revealed the Koran to him. Sophy Burnam describes his appearance: "His wings stretched from the east to the west. His feet were yellow, his wings green, and around his neck was a necklace of rubies. His face was of a radiant brightness. Between his two eyes it is written, 'THERE IS NO GOD BUT GOD, AND MUHAMMAD IS THE PROPHET OF GOD.'"

Cultures around the world have ancient references to mysterious winged beings. These creatures may vary from religion to religion and culture to culture, but they also have many things in common. Perhaps most important, they are messengers who bring tidings of hope from a world human beings cannot see.

Chapter 3

RELIGION & MODERN CULTURE

REPORTS
OF ANGELS TODAY

"Prime time spirituality has become popular, thanks to the success of *Touched by an Angel,*" says Leslie Moonves, president of CBS Entertainment, on a Web site called Hollywood Jesus. The show started in September of 1994 and featured two angels, Tess and Monica, who brought hope to people who have experienced tragedies. They also tried to show humans that God loves them. When the show first came out, *TV Guide's* reviewer wrote that it was dubious the show would be a success. He thought that before readers saw the review, the show might be off the air. The reviewer was wrong. For a time, *Touched by an Angel* was the highest-rated drama series on CBS. The producer of the show, Martha Williamson, believes firmly that angels are not just fairies flapping their wings, granting wishes like genies. She regards them as messengers of God, helping people and enabling them to understand the hard things that happen in life.

"The guardian angels of life sometimes fly so high as to be beyond our sight, but they are always looking down upon us."

—*Jean Paul Richter*

MODERN ACCOUNTS OF ANGELS

Reports of seeing angels are not just for television. Many people living in North America today claim angelic experiences. Some profess faith in traditional religions. Others are experimenting with alternative religions or exploring the *paranormal*. People who practice New-Age spirituality are especially interested in angels.

Sophy Burnham, author of *A Book of Angels*, believes the current popularity of angels is "because we have created this concept of God as punitive, jealous, judgmental," while "angels never are. They are utterly compassionate." Another reason why angels may have become so popular lately is the reaction against the *secularism* of Western society. "I think Americans in the '80s became weary of 20 years of materialism," says Burnham. "We were spiritually starved and hungry for some hope and inspiration. I think that's why *Angels* continue to be such a success." Evangelical Christians, devout Roman Catholics, and New Agers often disagree on matters of theology. Yet in each religion, some practitioners report angelic experiences.

As a child growing up in a very practical family, Sophy Burnham hardly gave angels a thought. Her father was a lawyer who did not believe in the supernatural, so Sophy was skeptical about celestial beings. At the age of twenty-eight that changed. She believes an angel saved her life.

It happened on a ski trip with her husband in France. Sophy rounded a curve on her skis, fell hard, and started sliding head first down the hill. She would have slid over the edge of a cliff—but a mysterious man

GLOSSARY

paranormal: Unable to be explained or understood in terms of scientific knowledge.

secularism: The belief that religion and religious institutions should have no part in political or civic affairs, or in running public institutions.

dressed in black seemed to come from nowhere, swooshed past her husband, who was looking on in horror, and blocked her slide. When she looked at him to thank him, the light in his eyes mesmerized her. She started to follow him down the trail, but he disappeared around a corner. In looking back on the incident years later, she came to the belief that he might have been an angel. Sophy went on to write *A Book of Angels*.

In *Heavenly Miracles*, Barbara Pitcavage writes in a similar fashion about how an angel saved her daughter's life. Mrs. Pitcavage had prayed that angels would protect her daughter Kathleen, a teenage driver. That same day, a driver swerved into Kathleen's lane, going ninety-five miles an hour from the opposite direction. His car collided with the driver's side of Kathleen's car. The door of her car, along with the seat belt, flew fifty feet (15 meters) away from the car. A paramedic said it was one of the worst accidents he had seen—the car had been sheered in half. A doctor said it was "divine intervention" that Kathleen was unhurt. Kathleen reported that she felt a hand reaching from behind, holding

ANGELS ARE UP NORTH TOO

In 2003, Ipsos-Reid, Canada's largest marketing research firm, conducted a major study on that nation's religious beliefs. The study found that 61 percent of Canadians believe in angels, and of those who do believe in angels, 26 percent reported they have had "personal experience with" angels. It is interesting to note that while Canadians are generally less "religious" than their neighbors to the south, the number of Canadians who believe in angels is almost the same as the number of U.S. residents with similar beliefs. Apparently, statistics regarding church attendance and belief in Christian doctrines have little effect on personal belief in divine messengers and protectors.

her firmly in place when the cars collided. Yet, there was no one behind her to do that.

ANGELIC GUIDANCE

Some people claim angels give people advance guidance that will protect them. Robert Smith is a former teacher and New-Age devotee who works with the Association of Research and Enlightenment (A.R.E), an

"Angels offer hope. Not each of us will receive a physical healing, miracle, or rescue when we want it, but a spiritual one."

—*Karen Goldman*

WHO WAS EDGAR CAYCE?

In many ways, Edgar Cayce was quite an ordinary man. He was a devoted husband and father, taught Sunday school, and enjoyed photography and gardening. One thing made him different from almost anyone in history—his psychic talents.

For more than forty years, Cayce spent time each day laying on a couch, hands folded over his stomach, and eyes closed in a self-induced sleep state. Questions sent in by his followers would be read to him, and a stenographer would take down his answers. A copy would be made for the files and the original sent to the questioner. History and science have confirmed many of the ideas contained in Cayce's psychic readings.

Cayce was more than a prognosticator, however. Decades before it became "popular," he extolled the importance of diet, attitudes, emotions, exercise, and the patient's role in the treatment of illness.

"What is it angels say when they show up with news? 'Fear not!'"

—*Martha Williamson*

organization committed to the teachings of psychic Edgar Cayce. In his book, *In the Presence of Angels*, Smith tells about Margaret Harmon, who was late for an appointment one day.

According to the book, Margaret Harmon was scurrying around getting ready for her appointment when she heard a voice telling her to go outside and fill her dog's water dish. Since she was late, she decided to do it when she got back home. She had walked outside to her car when she heard another urgent call from the same voice telling her to fill the dog's water dish. As Robert Smith relates the story, before that day she had never seen the water dish anywhere but beside the dog-house. That day, however, someone had placed the water dish just under the kitchen window. When she went to retrieve it, she smelled a strong odor of gas. She called the gas company, and they sent a worker immediately. The gas technician found a bad gas leak that would have caused a tremendous explosion if it had gone unnoticed much longer.

Some regard stories such as this as mere coincidences. Strange things happen all the time, but they are not necessarily supernatural. Others might say people like Harmon are especially sensitive to their feelings; their intuition tells them something is wrong. Believers in the paranormal might attribute such events to people having psychic abilities, so that premonitions reveal to them things that natural senses would not reveal. Others might combine views. They would point out that God—or God's angels—could certainly make use of humans' natural senses of intuition. Again, it is impossible to prove, disprove, or interpret reports of supernatural experiences in a way that makes sense to all points of view. Those who have such experiences often know what they believe happened; others are free to think what they will.

A PROFESSOR'S ACCOUNT OF VISIBLE ANGELS

In many accounts of angels and humans, people do not actually see the angel. However, sometimes they do. Sophy Burnham recounts a story in *The Day We Saw Angels,* written many years ago by S. Ralph Harlow, professor of Religion and Biblical Studies at Smith College in Northampton, Massachusetts.

WHAT DO ANGELS DO?

Sophy Burnham writes, "They rescue, give aid, anoint us with calm and serenity. They deliver messages of warning or of hope. They guide us, teach us, answer our prayers, and lead us to death. But always they are at the service of God, and not themselves."

According to the professor's account, the Harlows were taking a country walk in May, enjoying the welcome spring weather. As they walked, they heard muffled sounds of conversation behind them. Soon the sounds were close by—but amazingly, Harlow and his wife realized the voices were coming from overhead. Mr. Harlow wrote: "For about ten feet above us, and slightly to our left, was a floating group of glorious, beautiful creatures that glowed with spiritual beauty. We stopped and stared as they passed above us."

The Harlows could not understand their words. The angels did not look at the Harlows and soon passed beyond their sight. After the event, the Harlows questioned each other to make sure they both had seen the same thing. Though these angels were not in the woods to assist the Harlows in a specific way, the experience had a deep effect on them for the rest of their lives.

Science cannot prove angels are real—nor can it prove that they aren't. For believers, no amount of arguing can disprove them either. Bound by the material world of sight and sound and touch, human beings seem to crave stories of another world. Celestial messengers winging across the universe speak to people of a larger, wider world, a world filled with meaning and joy.

> *"An angel is a spiritual being, created by God without a body, for the servicedom of Christendom and the Church.*
>
> —*Martin Luther*

ANGEL UNAWARE

Roy Rogers and Dale Evans were a famous twentieth-century couple who made cowboy films for Republic Pictures. Audiences loved them for their singing skills, and for Roy's well-trained horse Trigger. But life for Roy and Dale was not always easy. Their only child was born with Down syndrome and died at age two. Out of their daughter's life and death came Dale's book, *Angel Unaware*, a bestseller that inspired a new perception of children with special needs. The book is still in print fifty years later. The title of the book refers to the verse in Hebrews 13:2: "Be not afraid to have strangers in your house, for some thereby have entertained angels unawares." Some angels may come to us in the guise of a child . . . a poor person . . . a person with special needs.

Chapter 4

MIRACLES IN SACRED SCRIPTURES

Thomas Jefferson, the third president of the United States, spent much of his leisure time writing a book, *The Morals of Jesus*. He clipped and pasted passages from the New Testament that he thought most closely told of the philosophy of Jesus Christ. In doing so, he left out all Jesus's miracles, including his miraculous birth and his resurrection from the dead. Jefferson felt that his more "scientific" portrayal of Jesus would be the wave of the future. Centuries later, if he were alive, he would be disappointed. Most Christians still read the Gospels with all the miracles still in them. In fact, those miracles are many Bible readers' favorite stories.

The same is true for Jews, Buddhists, and Muslims. Believers in many different religions recount stories of miracles; these are not just "extras" in the sacred texts. Miracles are essential expressions of the divine. In *The Book of Miracles*, Kenneth Woodward writes, "Miracles—and miracle workers—are found in all the major world religions. My contention is that without some knowledge of such stories and what they mean, no religion can be fully appreciated or understood."

MIRACLES OF THE BUDDHA

If one were to leave out the miracles surrounding Buddha, we would not have an account of his birth.

The man many of us know as the Buddha was born in 560 BCE. Buddhists refer to him as Shakyamuni Buddha, to distinguish him from followers who can become buddhas (enlightened ones) in their own right. He was a prince in Lumbini, Nepal, in the Himalayan ranges. When Buddha was conceived, his mother had a dream of a white elephant with six tusks entering her womb. When he was born, the child came painlessly out of her side. Buddha had achieved perfection in his former lives, and this was to be his last **rebirth**.

The first miracle of Buddha happened when he was just a toddler. His father thought Buddha should present himself in the temple to offer homage to the gods. When the little boy set his right foot in the temple, the account goes, all the statues of the gods rose and bowed down to him.

When he grew up, Buddha left the comfortable life of the palace. He went on a spiritual search and became an ascetic, a person who avoids physical comforts and pleasures in order to grow spiritually. The story goes that he spent six years in the forest with his legs crossed in a meditation pose. He only ate a single juniper berry and a single grain of rice.

GLOSSARY

conservative: In favor of keeping traditional values and customs, and against abrupt change.

fundamentalist: Someone who follows a literal interpretation of and strict adherence to a doctrine.

metaphorical: To use an object, word, or idea as a symbol for something else.

rebirth: The regeneration of something that has died or been destroyed.

He did not move the entire time. He sat through sun, rain, wind, mosquitoes, and snakes. He did not get up to urinate or lie down to sleep. When he was finished with his six years, he taught that extreme asceticism was futile. A middle-of-the-road approach was the better way.

Buddhism regards miracles somewhat differently from Western religions. In Judaism, Christianity, and Islam, God alone performs miracles by his own power. In Buddhism, however, according to the Buddha Dharma Education Association, the human mind is the source of miracles: "The development and purification of the mind through ethical and meditational training can unleash powers not normally apparent which would usually be described as miraculous."

Similar to other religions, followers of the various forms of Buddhism take differing approaches to the stories of miracles surrounding Shakyamuni Buddha. While some Buddhists take the stories literally,

"He therefore ministers to you the Spirit, and works miracles among you."

—Galatians 3:5

others understand the miracle accounts to be symbolic or ***metaphorical*** in nature. These Buddhists say the truth to which a story points— rather than the historical facts of the story—is what matters.

MIRACLES IN THE HEBREW BIBLE

God performs all the miracles in the Hebrew Bible. In the book of Exodus, for example, God did miraculous things to set his people, the Israelites, free from the oppression of the Egyptians. God spoke to Moses through a burning bush and directed Moses to go back to Egypt and set his people free from Pharaoh. God helped Moses perform miracles, and brought ten horrible plagues on the Egyptians until they let the Hebrews go. Then God parted the Red Sea so they could pass through it on foot. He guided them through the wilderness for many years, providing food and water, until they finally reached the Promised Land of Canaan.

According to Jewish tradition, Joshua led God's people after Moses's death. The ancient Hebrew writers recount his stories in the book of Joshua, including several miracles that occurred during Joshua's leadership. One was the famous Battle of Jericho, where the walls fell down after the Israelites marched around it seven times. Another was when Joshua and his army were fighting against the five Amorite kings. God threw the Amorites into confusion, attacked the soldiers with hailstones, and then made the sun stand still in answer to Joshua's prayer.

Jewish and Christian scholars take a variety of approaches to the miracle accounts in the Hebrew Bible. Rabbi Ken Spiro says, "God is certainly capable of doing whatever He likes, but He doesn't play around with the physical world and its workings. Therefore, most miracles are natural phenomena with awesomely good timing." At the same time, he says, "The Ten Plagues are a notable exception. Here the laws of nature are turned upside down to help free the Jews."

Other Bible scholars have suggested natural phenomena might have caused the ten plagues after all. Unusually heavy rains could cause the first nine of the ten, making the Nile River produce swarms of frogs, gnats, flies, and so on. However, the last plague—the death of the first-born—has no known natural explanation.

A scientific explanation has been presented for another miracle—the parting of the Red Sea. In 2003, Colin J. Humphreys, an honored Cambridge University physicist, published a book titled *The Miracles of Exodus.* He describes a rare natural event called "wind set-down," which could explain the parting of the Red Sea.

Scholars also have various interpretations of the miracle of the sun standing still for Joshua. If the earth stopped its rotation, even for a moment, it would disrupt gravity, wiping out everything—including human life. Even those who believe in miracles wonder why God would do something requiring such a vast reversal of natural laws. In 1918, a Protestant Christian scholar named Robert Dick Wilson, writing in the *Princeton Theological Review,* thoroughly studied the passage in Joshua. Looking at the words of the ancient text, Wilson concluded that the Bible author did not mean to say the sun "stopped." The passage actually says the sun was *eclipsed.* According to Wilson, a perfectly timed eclipse allowed Joshua's army to subdue their enemies.

According to these "natural" explanations of the miracles in the Hebrew Bible, God still performed miracles of a sort in each instance. He may not have changed the laws of nature, but instead caused natural events to happen at just the right moments. If "wind set-down" occurred for Moses, it happened just in time for Israel to escape from Egypt. As Wilson points out, Joshua's eclipse was also a marvelously

"If we could see the miracle of a single flower clearly, our whole life would change."

—*Shakyamuni Buddha*

well-timed answer to prayer. Jewish and Christian believers see God's hand behind what Rabbi Ken Spiro calls "awesomely good timing."

MIRACLES IN THE CHRISTIAN SCRIPTURES

Centuries later, the writers of the New Testament told about the life of Jesus Christ. According to Christian tradition, his birth itself was a miracle, since the scriptures say that his mother, Mary, was a virgin. An angel told her that she would conceive a child by the Holy Spirit and that this child would save his people from their sins. The virgin birth of Christ remains an important element of faith for most Christians today.

Miracles are a major part of the story of Jesus of Nazareth. Consider the percentage of space devoted in the Gospels to his miracles: 44 percent in Matthew, 65 percent in Mark, 29 percent in Luke, and more than 30 percent in John. There are exorcisms, nature miracles (such as calming storms, feeding five thousand people with only several fish and loaves of bread, changing water into wine, and walking on water), numerous healings, and three cases of people raised from the dead. Scholars disagree as to how the miracles happened and what they mean, but all agree they were a key part of Jesus's ministry.

Some New Testament scholars believe certain miracles performed by Jesus may have natural explanations. They ask if the "demons" in Mary Magdalene might have been schizophrenia, or if the "possessed boy" of Mark's Gospel may have suffered from epilepsy. The feeding of the five thousand has been explained as a "miracle" of sharing rather than multiplication—perhaps each person had a little bit hidden away, which Jesus moved them to share with others. Some New Testament scholars also suggest that the Gospel writers may have exaggerated some accounts of Jesus's miracles.

At the same time, many New Testament scholars today who are by no means *fundamentalists* still believe Jesus's miracles were more than merely natural events. Marcus Borg, one of today's best-known Jesus scholars, is not especially *conservative* in his beliefs; he does not regard the Bible as entirely inspired by God or free from error. At the same time, he writes in *The Meaning of Jesus*:

> In common with the majority of contemporary Jesus scholars, I see the claim that Jesus performed paranormal healings and ex- orcisms as history. . . . Indeed, more healing stories are told about Jesus than any other figure in the Jewish tradition. He must have been a remarkable healer." Borg defines Jesus's healings as para- normal, "meaning unusual . . . beyond the ordinary." He goes on to explain his belief that "inexplicable and remarkable things do happen; involving processes we do not understand . . . and Jesus seems to have been remarkably good at them.

In *The Interpreter's Dictionary of the Bible*, S. V. McCasland says, "If one believes in God, that God creates the universe . . . and controls it, most of the difficulties of miracles have thereby been dealt with. One who believes in God will believe in the possibility of miracles."

The central miracle of the New Testament is the resurrection of Jesus Christ. The Gospels relate that at the end of Jesus's life on earth, Roman soldiers crucified him in a most painful death. After three days, he rose from the dead and appeared to a number of his followers. According to Christian belief, this was not just resuscitation—like when one recovers from a drowning accident—it was a total reversal of death. It is vital to the Christian faith that Jesus still lives today.

A MIRACLE OF MOHAMMED

The Koran says that as Mohammad was traveling with his disciples, he had one of them go ahead to the village and scout out food and water. They met a woman on the way who had skins full of water. She told the scouts that the well was a day and a night's travel away. The men asked her to come with them to meet Mohammad, and she did. Mohammed ended up rubbing the mouth of her water skins—and then there was enough water for his entire troop and the skins still overflowed with water. Mohammad told his followers to bring the woman what food they had. When she returned to her village, she converted everyone to Islam.

Christian scholars who consider natural explanations for some New Testament miracles nonetheless tend to believe that the resurrection is a true and necessary miracle. Though they may disagree on some details, belief in the resurrection is vital for Christian faith. Saint Paul in his letter to the Corinthians makes clear just how important this event is to Christians: "If Christ has not been raised . . . then your faith is in vain" (1 Corinthians 15:14). C. S. Lewis, a writer and Oxford professor of the last century, described the resurrection this way: "Something perfectly new in the history of the Universe had happened. Christ had defeated death. The door which had always been locked had for the very first time been forced open."

"Miracles are not contrary to nature, but only contrary to what we know about nature."

—*Saint Augustine*

MIRACLES IN ISLAM

In the New Testament, Jesus is the primary figure performing miracles. In the Koran (sometimes spelled "Qur'an"), the Muslim sacred scriptures, Mohammad is not only a messenger of God's wisdom but also a worker of miracles. Although Mohammed performed miracles, they are not central to the Muslim faith as the miracles of Jesus are for Christians. A number of miracle stories center around producing water for thirsty people or for religious usage. Some tell of Mohammed providing food in time of need.

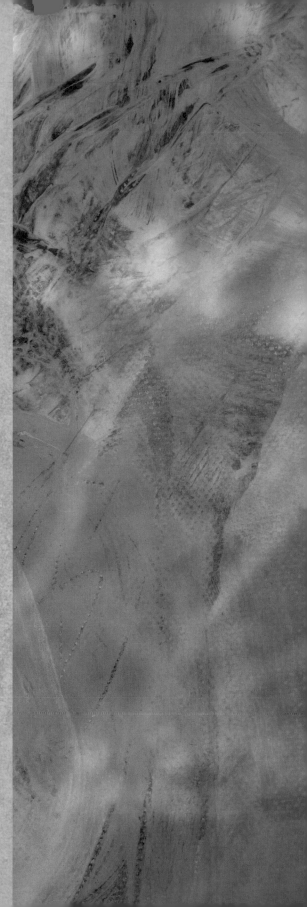

REPORTS OF MIRACLES TODAY

Duane Miller was a pastor. One Sunday morning as he was getting ready for church, he noticed that his throat was unusually sore. Soon the symptoms of the flu followed, but Duane did not let this keep him home. He loved to preach and sing, and he loved his church.

While at church that morning, his symptoms worsened. He was able to preach at the first service, but he could hardly sing. In her book *The Power of Miracles*, Joan Wester Anderson quotes Miller: "During my second sermon, every sound and inflection grated on the back of my throat like sandpaper." He went home to bed, and his flu took ten days to go away. Unfortunately, his throat did not recover. "It was painful and constricted, as if someone had my windpipe between his two fingers and was squeezing it whenever I swallowed. . . . There was a constant choking sensation. My voice was weak and hoarse."

He spent months visiting doctors who could not provide relief or healing. Eventually, Miller had to leave his church and sell his house. He was heartbroken at losing the *vocation* he loved, but he did not have a voice that would allow him to preach. At one point Duane asked, "What are you doing God? Don't you love me anymore? Have you abandoned me?"

Many doctors worked with Duane, photographing his throat and vocal chords. They were badly scarred. From the beginning, doctors documented every aspect of his illness. During the years, Duane had learned how to make his voice heard by using a guttural pressure and screaming at the top of his lungs.

His church asked him if he would teach his former Sunday school class. He was hesitant because of the uncomfortable sounds that were now his voice; who would want to listen? After pressure from friends, though, he decided that he would do it.

On the morning of January 17, 1993, Duane was teaching his class of two hundred people, using a microphone to amplify his hoarse voice. He was reading about God from Psalm 103, "Who forgives all your sins, Who heals all your diseases."

Duane said, "I was feeling no great faith—in fact, inside, I was still asking God, 'Why have You punished me this way?'" Duane addressed the group, "I've had, and you've had, *pit experiences*," and at the moment when he said, pit experiences, Duane felt something strange. It felt like the "hands" that had been locking his throat for three years had let go! He noticed something was different; his voice was stronger. The audience noticed right away. "Now . . . to say God doesn't do miracles today is to put God in a box, and God doesn't like to be put in a box," he said. Then he stopped, stunned. He could hear himself! His voice was normal! His wife ran up to him, and he broke down weeping. After Duane finished the lesson, the whole class broke out in a song: "Praise God from Whom All Blessings Flow!"

According to Anderson, the proof of this miracle is in the photographs. All the photos of Duane's throat after January 17, 1993, show smooth, healthy cords with no indication that any problem ever existed. All the scar tissue is gone—and doctors say that scar tissue does not just disappear. Duane Miller has published a book titled *Out of the Silence*. The book sells with a recording of the Sunday school lesson during which he recovered his voice. He believes it was a miracle of healing.

WHAT IS A MIRACLE?

What is a miracle? *Philosophers* and spiritual teachers have a variety of views regarding miracles, often based on great thinkers of the past.

The skeptic Benedict Spinoza defined a miracle as "a violation of natural law." Since he believed natural laws were unchangeable, Spinoza doubted the existence of all miracles. Likewise, the philosopher David

> *"Where there is great love there are always miracles."*
> —Willa Cather

Hume denied the possibility of miracles, arguing that science could not prove them. Most believers in miracles agree with Hume on that point—yet they say people can be rational and still believe in things that defy scientific proof. For example, one cannot weigh, measure, or quantify love. Science cannot prove that love exists, yet most people believe in it.

One of the worst definitions of a miracle may be that of the ancient Christian thinker Tertullian. He defined a miracle as something "absurd." Similarly, the medieval churchman Thomas Aquinas defined miracles as events "outside the order of nature," paving the way for the later *skepticism* of Hume.

In the fourth century, Saint Augustine said the opposite—that miracles are *not* contrary to nature. According to Augustine, nature is not just what we see on a regular basis. Everything God does—at any time and anywhere in the universe—is nature. Who would dare to claim he or she knows everything that God does everywhere? So, for Augustine, miracles are "natural" events, though they are less common than events we usually regard as natural.

In our postmodern age, many philosophers believe something similar to Augustine's view. It is common to speak of miracles as a part of "the unknown." Philosophers and many scientists now agree that science is unable to explain everything that takes place in our world and in the universe. Miracles are events that science cannot explain adequately, given our present understanding.

Spiritual teachers offer another definition of miracles, one based on the scriptures. The Bible and the Koran are not concerned whether certain events follow "the laws of nature." Such laws are a modern and scientific concept foreign to the scriptures. In the sacred writings, a

miracle is anything that points in a special way to the presence of God. Therefore, a miracle may be as extraordinary as the parting of the Red Sea or as ordinary as a spectacular sunset, if that sunset touches a person's soul in a powerful way.

Most of us are—to a greater or lesser degree—skeptical when we hear accounts of miracles. At the same time, we are also at least partially open to "the mysterious" intruding into our everyday lives. When a loved one recovers unexpectedly from illness, or when we see a mean-spirited person perform an unusually kind deed, we are tempted to believe that some greater power may have brushed against us. In the book *Divine Interventions*, the authors Dan Millman and Doug Childers write, "Within each of us lives a skeptic inclined toward reason—and a believer drawn to faith. When asked to choose between these two apparent opposites, the wise embrace both, seeing in each a necessary part of the whole."

"IT'S A MIRACLE": ACCOUNTS FROM THE TV SHOW

A reality-based TV series called *It's a Miracle* explores miraculous happenings. The show is about real-life accounts of healings, encounters, and interventions caused by unexplainable phenomena. The show centers on the mystery of miracles and how they change lives. Former host Richard Thomas selected stories from the show for a book, also titled *It's a Miracle.*

The story of Renay Poirer is one such example. While Renay, a senior electrician near Eau Claire, Wisconsin, was trying to repair a power outage at work, 100,000 volts of electricity charged through his body. The experience left him blind, and Renay's life was turned upside down. He had to find a new line of work, but although he tried, he couldn't hold down a job. The hardest part of the experience was not being able to see his two young daughters. He felt useless.

One day while riding in a car with a friend, a car on the side of the road flagged them down. A woman in the car needed CPR; she was having a heart attack. Renay saved the woman's life, and the experience helped Renay feel productive again. He went on to become a physical therapist assistant.

While he was at work one night, he got a severe, crushing headache. A brilliant light followed this feeling. All of a sudden, he could see. He ran down the hall to the chapel, dropped to his knees, and thanked God. He had been healed.

"To me every hour of the dark and light is a miracle. Every cubic inch of space is a miracle."
—*Walt Whitman*

THE SIGNS AND WONDERS MOVEMENT IN CHARISMATIC CHURCHES

During the past three decades of the twentieth century, charismatic Christian churches experienced tremendous growth in North America and throughout the world. Charismatics emphasize the power of the Holy Spirit in believers' lives. They may "speak in tongues," uttering words that are not in the English language, which they believe come directly from the spirit of God. Charismatics often emphasize the miraculous power of God to heal supernaturally. Such healing may be physical, emotional, or spiritual.

During the 1980s, the Vineyard churches, founded by Pastor John Wimber, emphasized what they called "Power Evangelism." They also called it the "Signs and Wonders" movement, after the New Testament terms for miraculous phenomena. Professors Charles Kraft and C. Peter Wagner, at nearby Fuller Seminary, also encouraged this movement. According to its supporters, Power Evangelism was a return to the methods of the very first Christians. Vineyard churches presented miraculous events in services, such as healings or deliverance from demons, as evidence of the power of Jesus Christ. The movement grew quickly for more than a decade. Wimber's embrace of the supernatural appealed to many Christians who were discontent with what they perceived as a gap between the wonder-working God of the Bible and the reality of many churches apparently void of supernatural experiences.

Christian psychiatrist John White became part of Wimber's Vineyard movement. In 1988, White wrote a book titled *When the Spirit*

Comes with Power, in which he describes his experiences of the miraculous in charismatic Christian circles. He admits, "My psychiatric experience is helpless before some of the phenomena I encountered." White then quotes from Puritan minister Jonathan Edwards:

> Persons of the greatest understanding . . . who had studied most about things of this nature, have been more confounded than others. Some such persons declare that all their former wisdom is brought to nought, and that they appear to have been babes, who knew nothing.

Some Christians felt the apparently supernatural events accompanying the Vineyards and other charismatic churches were signs of God moving in a new, powerful way in North America. Others expressed concern that the Vineyards were encouraging extreme behaviors and neglecting common-sense teaching of the Bible. In the mid-1990s, a portion of the Vineyard churches that were most heavily involved with signs and wonders broke away from the remainder of the denomination. Besides the Vineyards, many charismatic churches continue to emphasize signs and wonders.

SURROUNDED BY THE UNSEEN

Joan of Arcadia is another TV drama that touches on the miraculous. The miracle in this show is this: Joan, a totally normal teenager, sees and hears God speak to her in the form of various people who enter her life. She never knows who is going to turn up next as God: it might be a cute boy her own age, or the lunch woman, or a little girl. *Joan of Arcadia* gives an earthy twist to the normally unseen spiritual world. Karen Armstrong wrote, "One of the reasons religion seems irrelevant today is that many of us no longer have the sense that we are surrounded by the unseen." *Joan of Arcadia* restores that sense to many viewers.

THE LOURDES OF AMERICA

Catholics attribute many miracles to the Virgin Mary. She is supposed to have made a famous appearance in Lourdes, France, in 1858. Now there is a place people call "The Lourdes of the United States." Veronica Lueken, a middle-aged mother of five, had her first vision of the Virgin Mary in Bayside, Queens, on April 7, 1970. The appearance, or "apparition," occurred in her home. Mary told Leuken that she would appear on the grounds of the church nearby—St. Robert Bellarmine Church—on June 18, 1970. The Virgin told her to hold prayer vigils on that day. The Virgin also wished a shrine to be built, dedicated to Our Lady of the Roses, Mary, helper of Mothers. Leuken says Mary has been appearing to her ever since then. The church has moved the shrine to the old World Fair's grounds to make room for all the people who come every year. The Catholic Church has never approved these apparitions or any other visions of the Virgin in the United States in the twentieth century. However, thousands of faithful pilgrims continue to believe.

"A belief in miracles is not a vacation from reason. . . . Not only is it reasonable to believe that miracles can and do happen, it is unreasonable to think they cannot and do not occur."

Sometimes miraculous events convey a sense of where to go or a special knowledge about life. In the book *Heavenly Miracles*, Teri Brinsley describes a miracle of knowledge imparted to her husband.

David never knew his father, who left the family before David was out of diapers, but all his life, David had a burning desire to meet his father. In October of 1994, as David and his wife attended their regular church, David's wife noticed that a Bible in the pew ahead of them had a woman's name that matched David's father's last name—Lambert. After a few moments of conversation with the woman after church, David realized that this woman, Maria Lambert, was his half sister. She put David in touch with his father. Maria had been seated across the aisle when she felt a strong urge to move to the other side of the sanctuary—right in front of David. She had wondered why she was moving. If she had not gone with her feeling, David might never have found his father.

In the film *Contact*, Dr. Ellie Arroway says, "I had an experience. I can't prove it . . . I can't even explain it, but everything that I know as a human being, everything I am, tells me that it was real. I was given something wonderful, something that changed me forever." She speaks for many people in today's culture who have had extraordinary experiences.

Ralph M. McInerny, a professor of philosophy at Notre Dame University, says, "A belief in miracles is not a vacation from reason. . . . Not only is it reasonable to believe that miracles can and do happen, it is unreasonable to think they cannot and do not occur."

Chapter 6

DEMONS IN SACRED SCRIPTURES

People today are not only obsessed with angels and miracles, positive expressions of the supernatural world; many people are also fascinated by demons, evil spirits with the power to act in the physical world.

"For they are the spirits of devils, working miracles, which go forth unto the kings of the earth and of the whole world."

—Revelation 16:14

DEMONS IN BUDDHISM

Mara the king of demons went to the place where the Blessed One (Shakyamuni Buddha) was. Mara addressed the Blessed One saying, "Thou art bound by all fetters, human and divine. Thou art bound by strong fetters. Thou wilt not be delivered from me!"

Buddha replied, "I am delivered from all fetters, human and divine. I am delivered from the strong fetters. Thou art struck down, O Death."

Then Mara said, "The fetter which fills the sky, with which mind is bound, with that fetter I will bind thee. Thou wilt not be delivered from me."

Buddha answered, "Whatever forms, sounds, odors, flavors, or contacts there are which please the senses, in me desire for them has ceased. Thou art struck down, O Death."

Mara the wicked one understood. "The Blessed One knows me, the perfect One knows me." Then, sad and afflicted, he vanished.

This exchange comes from an ancient record of the life of the Buddha. The word translated as "demon" in Buddhist writings is the **Sanskrit** word meaning "bringer of death."

According to Buddhism, there are four kinds of demons:

1. demons that are afflictions
2. demons that are illnesses
3. the demon of death
4. heavenly demons

One goal in Buddhist spirituality is to escape from feelings of attachment to material things. When a person has freed herself from chasing after material things, and when she has gained spiritual enlightenment, evil beings cannot influence her.

SATAN IN THE HEBREW BIBLE

The Torah and other Jewish writings refer to Satan; the English translation of the Hebrew word for Satan would be "adversary" or "accuser." The figure of Satan is found in three places in the Hebrew Bible: Job 1–2, Zechariah 3:1–2, and 1 Chronicles 21:1. In the first two, Satan appears as a member of God's court who accuses human beings before God. He is not yet an enemy of God or the leader of demonic forces. In

RELIGION & MODERN CULTURE

"Millions of spiritual creatures walk the earth
Unseen. . . ."

    —*John Milton,* Paradise Lost

Genesis, we read about the serpent that tempted Eve, but the Old Testament never refers to the serpent as Satan. In the book of Job, Satan functions like a prosecutor who is acting against Job. However, God limits Satan by establishing boundaries for him: Satan can use disease to attack Job, but cannot take his life. In 1 Chronicles 21:1, Satan has a proper name and acts as a tempter. He is hostile and harmful. Yet here, also, God limits Satan's power.

    The book of Genesis, chapter six, says, "The sons of God [Nephilim] saw that the daughters of men were fair; and they took to wife such of them as they chose." The Bible does not say exactly who these "sons of God" were. Interpreters have surmised they were fallen angels. Genesis goes on to say, "The Nephilim were on the earth in those days." Readers have assumed the Nephilim were the offspring of angels and mortal wives. Later Jewish mystical writings, such as the book of Enoch and certain Dead Sea Scrolls, tell more about this event. They describe a race of angels called the Watchers, created by God to assist in his work of creation. The Watchers intermarried with humans, creating a race of evil giants. The book of Enoch explains that the angels taught men to make weapons and war.

    Jewish **rabbinic literature** has two accounts telling how Satan came to be. The first account is that God created him on the same day as Eve—the sixth day. The story goes that he had a role in humanity's **Fall**. The second account is that Satan is a fallen angel. Satan is connected with the "evil impulse" within man called *Yetzer ha Ra*. This evil impulse allows Satan to work his will against humanity. The general belief is that a group of satans work with a chief Satan; the book of Enoch tells of five satans. The first and second satans are said to have been re-

84

"Devils are depicted with bats' wings and good angels with birds' wings . . . because most men like birds better than bats."

—*C. S. Lewis*

RELIGION & MODERN CULTURE

sponsible for leading the angels astray and for bringing them down to earth, where they sinned with the daughters of men. The third satan brought about the fall of Adam and Eve. These satans are allowed to access heaven in order to accuse human beings, but they are not confined to heaven. The rabbinical writings also talk of the eventual destruction of the evil angels.

DEMONS IN THE CHRISTIAN NEW TESTAMENT

The Christian New Testament portrays Satan as the source of evil and destruction. The Christian Bible also names him Belial, Beelzebub, and the devil. According to the Gospels, Jesus spent forty days and nights fasting in the desert, where the devil came and tempted him (but Jesus did not give in to temptation). The first four books of the New Testament, the Gospels, also present both demons and Satan as being able to possess individuals.

Luke 10:18 mentions the final destruction of Satan. Jesus says, "I saw Satan fall like lightning from heaven." Matthew 25:41 also describes the fate of evil beings. At the last judgment, Jesus says to the wicked, "Depart from me, you who are cursed, into the eternal fire prepared for the devil and his angels."

"Devil is the opposite of angel only as Bad Man is the opposite of Good Man."

—*C. S. Lewis*

THE DEVIL ACCORDING TO ISLAM

Muslims throw stones at the devil. They have a custom of throwing seven pebbles at a stone pillar that represents the evil one. When God told Abraham to sacrifice his son, the devil tried to argue with him against doing it, but Abraham threw stones at the devil. Today, *pilgrims* travel to Mina to do this. After they throw stones, they sacrifice a lamb.

According to Islam Online:

> The devil is a real malicious enemy to mankind in general and Muslims in particular; he wants to fetter and chain them with sins and disobedience and to do what may invalidate their pilgrimage through whispering to them as he tried to whisper to Prophet Abraham (Ibrahim), peace and blessing be upon him. Satan does this only out of his anger and dissatisfaction of the mercies being showered on the pilgrims on that solemn occasion.

The Koran tells the story of how God first made angels to worship and praise God. Next, God made humans and told the angels to serve them. However, Satan (Iblis) loved God more than he loved all the angels, and he refused to bow down to them. This angered God, and he told Satan to get out of his sight. God cast the angel into hell immediately. According to Islam, angels fell after humans were made; Christianity says angels fell before the creation of humans.

Islam describes a class of beings created for evil. They are the shaitans. The story goes that one shaitan, a great-grandson of Iblis, was taught certain chapters of the Koran. This was taking a step toward happiness. Only in Islam is an evil being able to improve itself.

THE DEVIL DEFEATED BY HUMILITY

Once some people came to a saintly old man in Thebaid. They brought a man possessed by a demon, hoping the old man would cure him. They asked him persistently for quite some time. The old man finally said to the demon, "Go out of God's creation." The demon replied, "'I will go out, but let me ask you just one thing. Tell me, who are the goats and who are the sheep?" Then the old man said, "A goat is someone such as I am. But as for the sheep, well, only God knows." Hearing this, the demon cried out in a loud voice, "Look, because of your humility I am going out!" Moreover, he went away that very moment.

—A fable told by fourth-century Christian hermits

Chapter 7

REPORTS
OF DEMONS TODAY

When someone insults Nancy, she hears voices in her head telling her to kill the offender. She prays this will go away, but to no avail. Nancy needs to:

1. cut back on coffee
2. get professional help for her dissociative identity disorder
3. see an exorcist
4. all the above

This tongue-in-cheek quiz opens an article in the September 2001 issue of *Christianity Today* magazine. In the twenty-first century, more Americans than ever before are choosing option number three. Half a century ago, belief in Satan and demons reached an all-time low, but in past decades belief in evil spirits—and in deliverance from evil spirits—has increased steadily.

Some observers believe that in the past few decades the media has changed public attitudes toward demonic influences. In 1973, the movie *The Exorcist* was hugely popular. The writers claimed they based the movie on an actual exorcism that occurred in 1949. Popular television shows such as the *X-Files, Buffy the Vampire Slayer, Angel,* and *Charmed* may have also increased public belief in demons. In 1983, psychiatrist M. Scott Peck published a book titled *People of the Lie.* In this book, Peck expressed his belief in the possessing power of evil and the counteracting power of religious exorcisms. This endorsement by a mental health professional helped ***deliverance ministry*** gain respectability.

Some evangelicals regard C. Fred Dickason as a leading authority on evil spirits. Dickason believes the popularity of movies like *The Exorcist* was "more a symptom than a cause" of the deliverance phenomena. In the 1960s, when Dickason was teaching a course on "angelology" at Moody Bible Institute in Chicago, the school began getting calls from people who had dabbled in the occult and believed they were demon possessed. The school forwarded these calls to Dickason. He says he "had to learn

GLOSSARY

deliverance ministry: Religious practice in which people are freed from demonic influence.

placebo effect: A sense of benefit that a patient feels that comes only from the knowledge that treatment has been given.

in a hurry" how to deliver people from evil spirits. Since then, Dickason and his wife have counseled more than six hundred people with demonic problems.

It is hard to say how many Protestant Christian ministries deal in deliverance from evil spirits; the number is well over a thousand. The Roman Catholic Church has also increased its supply of exorcists. In 1955, only two Catholic priests were authorized to do exorcisms in the United States; there are around twenty now. Robert Barron, a spokesperson on exorcisms for the Catholic Diocese of Chicago, says, "People are more willing to entertain the possibility of the supernatural," now than they were in the past.

SOME ARE SKEPTICAL

Of course, many—including pastors and priests—are skeptical regarding evil spirits. Dissociative identity disorder (DID), a mental illness formerly labeled multiple personality disorder (MPD), describes a condition

SIGNS OF DEMONIC INFLUENCE IN A PERSON'S LIFE

What are the signs of demonization? Those who deal with such things disagree with one another.

At one extreme, a small minority of ministers attribute almost any problem to demons. They blame demons for headaches, watching pornography, tiredness, anger, jealousy, fear, and nervousness. They even blame common illnesses on evil spirits.

At the other extreme, the Roman Catholic Church will only do an exorcism if four conditions for demonization are met: supernatural power, fierce hatred of holy things, supernatural knowledge, and the ability to speak in languages the person has not previously learned. Ninety-five percent of people who apply for Catholic Church exorcisms fail to meet these criteria.

Most Christians, in both Catholic and Protestant camps, have views regarding evidence of the devil at work that fall between these two extremes. They believe demons may influence the lives of ordinary believers, but they do not see evil spirits at work everywhere.

"The devil's most devilish when respectable."
—*Elizabeth Barrett Browning*

where an individual has two or more selves, or "alters." Psychologists—some evangelical Christians included—are concerned that deliverance ministries may mistake cases of DID for demon possession. Considerable psychological harm might result from such a mistaken diagnosis.

The Committee for the Scientific Investigation of Claims of the Paranormal researched the original case that inspired *The Exorcist.* They conclude that the book and movie greatly exaggerated that case. Their report concludes:

> It certainly is true that exorcisms have been (and continue to be) performed, often on emotionally and mentally disturbed people. Whether those undergoing the exorcism are truly possessed by spirits or demons is another matter entirely. Most often, exorcisms are done on people of strong religious faith. To the extent that exorcisms 'work,' it is primarily due to the power of suggestion and the ***placebo*** effect. If you believe you are possessed, and that a given ritual will cleanse you, then it just might.

Among Christians, some are skeptical of the deliverance "fad." In the *Reformation and Revival Journal,* Pastor Steve Fernandez writes, "The entire deliverance theology is built on the false premise that believers can be demon-possessed, and this, in turn, is based on a faulty view of faith and the work of the Spirit that occurs in conversion."

RELIGION & MODERN CULTURE

"The Devil is an optimist if he thinks he can make people worse than they are."

—*Karl Kraus, Austrian writer*

MANY BELIEVERS SAY DELIVERANCE HAS HELPED THEM

As a *Christianity Today* article by Clinton E. Arnold attests, "undeniably, some people have been helped by exorcism and deliverance." Arnold tells about Michael Easton, a fifty-four-year-old businessperson. He converted to Christianity in 1979, but that "did not stop him from multipartner homosexuality, alcoholism, and a drug habit." In 1987, Easton's alcoholism was completely out of control. He went to a deliverance meeting in Montana led by visiting pastor Win Worley. Worley prayed for Easton for more than half an hour. During that time, Easton says he experienced "deep, heavy coughing, lots of tears, things coming out of my nose, and a substance that came out of my stomach—it's just as if a faucet was turned on." Since that day, more than fifteen years ago, Michael Easton says he has not engaged in any risky sexual acts, has stopped smoking pot, and has not touched alcohol.

Neil Anderson is another popular writer and speaker on the topic of spiritual warfare. One of his clients was a public school district superintendent. In Anderson's book *The Bondage Breaker*, this former client writes, "I contacted you because I had been experiencing a host of seemingly inexplicable 'psychologically related' attacks. . . . I seriously questioned the purpose of life. I experienced horrible nightmares which woke me up screaming." Anderson helped this man find deliverance. The letter goes on to say, "Since our meeting, I haven't had one nightmare. Neil, I'm afraid there are many Christians like me out there leading lives of 'quiet desperation' due to the attack of demonic forces. If I can fall prey to these forces . . . so can others."

Speakers and writers who believe in deliverance ministry emphasize that demons cannot actually "possess" a person who has given his or her life to Christ. They point out that the New Testament, in its original Greek language, uses the term *daemonizo*—literally, "influenced by a demon." Thus, they speak of "demonization" rather than "possession." However, most people in the English-speaking world understand "possession" and "demonization" as meaning the same thing.

BELIEVERS SAY DELIVERANCE IS A SPIRITUAL—NOT PHYSICAL—STRUGGLE

Some ministers attempt to physically restrain people with evil spirits. Such techniques have had horrific consequences. People have died from choking and other injuries sustained during deliverances that involved physical restraint. Fortunately, these incidents have been rare.

DEMONS REPORTED IN CANADA ALSO

Though social scientists regard Canada as being less "religious" than the United States, that seems to have little effect in some areas of spiritual belief and practice. Canadians believe in angels and demons almost as much as their U.S. counterparts do. A January 2002 CBC news story reports widespread interest in deliverance ministries in Canada. A psychiatrist at an Ottawa clinic interviewed for the article says a third of his clients have tried deliverance as a cure for their mental problems.

"Put on all of God's armor so that you will be able to stand against all strategies and tricks of the Devil."

—Ephesians 6:10

Both Neil Anderson and C. Fred Dickason believe that deliverance from demons is not a physical conflict. Dickason, quoted in *Christianity Today,* says, "Spiritual warfare confrontation and dismissal of evil spirits are done by the Lord Jesus. We're only facilitators to the situation. And since we're counseling the entire person, we're not there primarily to confront the spirits; we are trying to clear up some problems in people's lives by getting them to recognize truth and apply it to their lives." Neil Anderson takes a similar approach. He says, "It's a truth encounter

DEMONS IN LITERATURE

Stories of spiritual beings that defy God and good in the world have been a subject of great interest for poets and authors for thousands of years. Italian poet Dante Alighieri wrote of hell (and how you got there) in his *The Divine Comedy* (c. 1306). The work of poet and artist William Blake (1757–1827) often reflected demons and angels that appeared in his visions. Even poet Percy Bysshe Shelley occasionally wrote about demons.

Perhaps one of the most often told stories about demons concerns Dr. Faust. It is believed that the original tale came from a German story, with some basis in fact. In 1604, British author Christopher Marlowe wrote a play—*The Tragical History of Doctor Faustus*. Perhaps the best-known telling of the Faust story is Johann Wolfgang von Goethe's *Faust*. Both tell the story of Faust, who sells his soul to the devil in return for having the devil serve him.

A QUESTION OF PARADIGMS?

A "paradigm" is a term used to describe the way individuals look at reality; a paradigm is a set of beliefs about how the world works. Ultimately, our paradigms determine how we perceive reality. They are the building blocks for our worldview.

In the New Testament world, no one looked at human reality in terms of psychological processes; this particular paradigm would not arrive on the scene for more than a thousand years. Instead, people explained human phenomena in terms of spiritual forces. The paradigm helped them confront and handle the reality they faced.

Today, however, most of us have been influenced by psychology's paradigms—and we in turn use them to help us confront and handle reality. For many of us, psychology "works."

But the spiritual paradigm also "works" for many other individuals. Some philosophers theorize that reality is something that exists unchanged beyond all paradigms; it's merely the paradigms—and the words we use to describe those paradigms—that change. In other words, psychological vocabulary does not describe "ultimate truth" any more than spiritual vocabulary does.

"Spiritual reality is at the heart of everything."
—*Walter Wink*

rather than a power encounter." Anderson begins a deliverance session by asking the person to affirm the power of Christ to help her and affirming that the Bible is God's truth. He commands the spirits *not* to reveal themselves so he can work with the person seeking freedom. He says, "The goal in helping people find freedom in Christ is to avoid all activity which would short-circuit their ability to participate in the process." Anderson also teaches the person seeking deliverance to pray "warfare prayers" on his own. This way, the afflicted person recognizes it is the power of God—not Neil Anderson or any other minister—freeing him from evil spirits.

KEEPING DEMONS IN PERSPECTIVE

Even among religious believers, there is a variety of perspectives on demons. Oxford professor C. S. Lewis once said, "There are two equal and opposite errors into which our race can fall about the devils. One is to disbelieve in their existence. The other is to believe, and to feel an excessive and unhealthy interest in them." As is the case with many other things, the truth seems to lie between the extremes.

Long ago, in the Egyptian desert, a hermit came to speak with Abbot Pambo. He asked the abbot, "How come the devils keep me from doing good to my neighbor?" Pambo scolded him, "Don't talk like that! Is God a liar? Why not just admit that you don't want to be merciful? Didn't God say long ago, 'I have given you power to tread upon serpents and scorpions and on all the forces of the enemy'? So why don't you just stamp out the evil spirit?" Those who believe in demons can still find wisdom in these ancient words.

Anderson, Joan Wester. *The Power of Miracles: Stories of God in the Everyday.* New York: Ballantine, 1998.

Anderson, Neil T. *The Bondage Breaker.* New York: Harvest House, 1990.

Burnham, Sophy. *A Book of Angels.* New York: Ballantine, 1990.

Miller, Jamie C., Laura Lewis, and Jennifer Basye Sander. *Heavenly Miracles: Magical True Stories of Guardian Angels and Answered Prayers.* New York: HarperCollins, 2000.

Nickell, Joe. *Looking for a Miracle: Weeping Icons, Relics, Stigmata, Visions & Healing Cures.* New York: Prometheus, 1993.

Thomas, Richard. *It's a Miracle: Real-Life Inspirational Stories Based on the Pax TV Series It's a Miracle.* New York: Doubleday, 2002.

Woodward, Kenneth L. *The Book of Miracles: The Meaning of the Miracle Stories in Christianity, Judaism, Buddhism, Hinduism, and Islam.* New York: Simon & Schuster, 2000.

FOR MORE INFORMATION

The Angel Quiz
www.leaderu.com/orgs/probe/
docs/angel-q.html

Angels and Miracles
www.ainglkiss.com/miracles

Catholic Encyclopedia—Angels
www.newadvent.org

Deliverance from Demons
patriot.net/~bmcgin/
deliverance.html

Demonology
www.djmcadam.com/
demons.htm

Dharma Talks.com
www.dharmatalks.com/
xmass_story.htm

God's Tiny Miracles
www.embracedbythelight.com/
miracles/index.htm

I Believe in Angels.com
www.ibelieveinangels.com

Mysteries from Heaven
www.members.aol.com/
BILLANDEB/Angels.html

Spirit Home.com
www.spirithome.com

Publisher's note:
The Web sites listed on this page were active at the time of publication.
The publisher is not responsible for Web sites that have changed their
addresses or discontinued operation since the date of publication. The
publisher will review and update the Web-site list upon each reprint.

PICTURE CREDITS

The illustrations in RELIGION AND MODERN CULTURE are photo montages made by Dianne Hodack. They are a combination of her original mixed-media paintings and collages, the photography of Benjamin Stewart, various historical public-domain artwork, and other royalty-free photography collections.

AUTHORS: Kenneth and Marsha McIntosh are former teachers. They have two children, Jonathan, nineteen, and Eirené, sixteen. Marsha has a bachelor's of science degree in Bible and education, and Kenneth has a bachelor's degree in English education and a master's degree in theology. They live in Flagstaff, Arizona, with their children, a dog, and two cats. Kenneth frequently speaks on topics of religion and society.

CONSULTANT: Dr. Marcus J. Borg is the Hundere Distinguished Professor of Religion and Culture in the Philosophy Department at Oregon State University. Dr. Borg is past president of the Anglican Association of Biblical Scholars. Internationally known as a biblical and Jesus scholar, the *New York Times* called him "a leading figure among this generation of Jesus scholars." He is the author of twelve books, which have been translated into eight languages. Among them are *The Heart of Christianity: Rediscovering a Life of Faith* (2003) and *Meeting Jesus Again for the First Time* (1994), the best-selling book by a contemporary Jesus scholar.

CONSULTANT: Dr. Robert K. Johnston is Professor of Theology and Culture at Fuller Theological Seminary in Pasadena, California, having served previously as Provost of North Park University and as a faculty member of Western Kentucky University. The author or editor of thirteen books and twenty-five book chapters (including *The Christian at Play*, 1983; *The Variety of American Evangelicalism*, 1991; *Reel Spirituality: Theology and Film in Dialogue*, 2000; *Life Is Not Work/Work Is Not Life: Simple Reminders for Finding Balance in a 24/7 World*, 2000; *Finding God in the Movies: 33 Films of Reel Faith*, 2004; and *Useless Beauty: Ecclesiastes Through the Lens of Contemporary Film*, 2004), Johnston is the immediate past president of the American Theological Society, an ordained Protestant minister, and an avid bodysurfer.